W9-CLH-947

Your Government:
How It Works

The Electoral College

Martha S. Hewson

Chelsea House Publishers
Philadelphia

Purchased with funds from the
Allegheny Regional Asset District

CHELSEA HOUSE PUBLISHERS
Editor in Chief Sally Cheney
Director of Production Kim Shinners
Creative Manager Takeshi Takahashi
Manufacturing Manager Diann Grasse

Staff for THE ELECTORAL COLLEGE
Editor Colleen Sexton
Production Assistant Jaimie Winkler
Picture Researcher Jaimie Winkler
Series Designers Keith Trego, Takeshi Takahashi
Cover Designer Terry Mallon
Layout 21st Century Publishing and Communications, Inc.

First Printing
1 3 5 7 9 8 6 4 2

Library of Congress Cataloging-in-Publication Data

Hewson, Martha S.
      The electoral college / by Martha S. Hewson.
          p. cm. — (Your government—how it works)
      Includes bibliographical references and index.
       ISBN 0-7910-6790-4
       1. Electoral college—United States—Juvenile literature—
History. 2. Electoral college—United States—Juvenile literature.
3. Presidents—United States—Election—Juvenile literature—
History. 4. Presidents—United States—Election—Juvenile
literature. [1. Electoral college. 2. Presidents—Election.] I. Title.
II. Series.
JK529 .H48 2002
324.6'3'0973—dc21
                                                    2001007914

Dedication: For Jackie Ziegler and Craig Ziegler, with many thanks
for sharing your knowledge of history and the law.

Contents

YOUR GOVERNMENT HOW IT WORKS

Introduction

Government: Crises of Confidence

Arthur M. Schlesinger, jr.

FROM THE START, Americans have regarded their government with a mixture of reliance and mistrust. The men who founded the republic understood the importance of government. "If men were angels," observed the 51st Federalist Paper, "no government would be necessary." But men are not angels. Because human beings are subject to wicked as well as to noble impulses, government was deemed essential to assure freedom and order.

The American revolutionaries, however, also knew that government could become a source of injury and oppression. The men who gathered in Philadelphia in 1787 to write the Constitution therefore had two purposes in mind: They wanted to establish a strong central authority and to limit that central authority's capacity to abuse its power.

To prevent the abuse of power, the Founding Fathers wrote two basic principles into the Constitution. The principle of federalism divided power between the state governments and the central authority. The principle of the separation of powers subdivided the central authority itself into three branches—the executive, the legislative, and the judiciary—so that "each may be a check on the other."

YOUR GOVERNMENT: HOW IT WORKS examines some of the major parts of that central authority, the federal government. It explains how various officials, agencies, and departments operate and explores the political organizations that have grown up to serve the needs of government.

The federal government as presented in the Constitution was more an idealistic construct than a practical administrative structure. It was barely functional when it came into being.

This was especially true of the executive branch. The Constitution did not describe the executive branch in any detail. After vesting executive power in the president, it assumed the existence of "executive departments" without specifying what these departments should be. Congress began defining their functions in 1789 by creating the Departments of State, Treasury, and War.

President Washington, assisted by Secretary of the Treasury Alexander Hamilton, equipped the infant republic with a working administrative structure. Congress also continued that process by creating more executive departments as they were needed.

Throughout the 19th century, the number of federal government workers increased at a consistently faster rate than did the population. Increasing concerns about the politicization of public service led to efforts—bitterly opposed by politicians—to reform it in the latter part of the century.

The 20th century saw considerable expansion of the federal establishment. More importantly, it saw growing impatience with bureaucracy in society as a whole.

The Great Depression during the 1930s confronted the nation with its greatest crisis since the Civil War. Under Franklin Roosevelt, the New Deal reshaped the federal government, assigning it a variety of new responsibilities and greatly expanding its regulatory functions. By 1940, the number of federal workers passed the 1 million mark.

Critics complained of big government and bureaucracy. Business owners resented federal regulation. Conservatives worried about the impact of paternalistic government on self-reliance, on community responsibility, and on economic and personal freedom.

When the United States entered World War II in 1941, government agencies focused their energies on supporting the war effort. By the end of World War II, federal civilian employment had risen to 3.8 million. With peace, the federal establishment declined to around 2 million in 1950. Then growth resumed, reaching 2.8 million by the 1980s.

A large part of this growth was the result of the national government assuming new functions such as: affirmative action in civil rights, environmental protection, and safety and health in the workplace.

Some critics became convinced that the national government was a steadily growing behemoth swallowing up the liberties of the people. The 1980s brought new intensity to the debate about government growth. Foes of Washington bureaucrats preferred local government, feeling it more responsive to popular needs.

But local government is characteristically the government of the locally powerful. Historically, the locally powerless have often won their human and constitutional rights by appealing to the national government. The national government has defended racial justice against local bigotry, upheld the Bill of Rights against local vigilantism, and protected natural resources from local greed. It has civilized industry and secured the rights of labor organizations. Had the states' rights creed prevailed, perhaps slavery would still exist in the United States.

Americans are still of two minds. When pollsters ask large, spacious questions—Do you think government has become too involved in your lives? Do you think government should stop regulating business?—a sizable majority opposes big government. But when asked specific questions about the practical work of government—Do you favor Social Security? Unemployment compensation? Medicare? Health and safety standards in factories? Environmental protection?—a sizable majority approves of intervention.

We do not like bureaucracy, but we cannot live without it. We need its genius for organizing the intricate details of our daily lives. Without bureaucracy, modern society would collapse. It would be impossible to run any of the large public and private organizations we depend on without bureaucracy's division of labor and hierarchy of authority. The challenge is to keep these necessary structures of our civilization flexible, efficient, and capable of innovation.

More than 200 years after the drafting of the Constitution, Americans still rely on government but also mistrust it. These attitudes continue to serve us well. What we mistrust, we are more likely to monitor. And government needs our constant attention if it is to avoid inefficiency, incompetence, and arbitrariness. Without our informed participation, it cannot serve us individually or help us as a people to attain the lofty goals of the Founding Fathers.

Texas governor George W. Bush (left) and Vice President Al Gore faced off in the 2000 presidential election. In the end, the race for the presidency came down to a battle for Florida's electoral votes.

CHAPTER 1

The 2000 Election: Bush vs. Gore

TEXAS GOVERNOR GEORGE W. BUSH had plans for election night. He and his family would go out to dinner at an Austin restaurant. Then they would join friends and campaign staff in a hotel suite, where they would watch the election returns on television. As the Republican Party's candidate for president, Bush hoped that by the end of the night, he'd be declared the winner of the 2000 election.

But during dinner, the television networks began reporting that Vice President Al Gore, the Democratic Party's candidate, was winning in the states of Michigan and Florida. This was not a good sign for the Bush campaign. Bush's brother, Jeb, was especially concerned. He was the governor of Florida and had promised to deliver the state's votes for his older brother. Bush abruptly changed his plans for the evening. The family left the restaurant and headed back to the Texas governor's mansion. If Bush was going to lose, he wanted to be at home with his family.

If you had been watching television that night, you would have seen a large map of the United States on the screen. Throughout the evening, the networks constantly projected which states would choose which candidate. But why was there so much emphasis on the states? The states themselves weren't voting. Didn't the people elect the president?

As the networks constantly reminded viewers that night, the key to any presidential election lies not in the **popular vote,** but in the electoral college. The popular vote is the total number of votes cast by the people. But the U.S. Constitution says that the president is to be chosen not by the people, but by electors. When people vote, they are not really voting for a candidate, but for a slate, or list, of **electors** who have pledged to vote for that candidate in the electoral college. At the state level, each political party selects a slate of electors. If a party's candidate wins the state's popular vote, then the electors from that party participate in the electoral college. The electors meet in December to cast their votes. Each state has the same number of electoral votes as it has senators and representatives in Congress. Washington, D.C., also has three votes, bringing the total number of electoral votes to 538. To win, a candidate must receive an **absolute majority,** or one over half of the total, which is at least 270 votes. If no candidate has an absolute majority, the election is decided by the U.S. House of Representatives.

In most states, the candidate who wins the state's popular vote is awarded all of that state's electoral votes. So on election night 2000, both campaigns were busy keeping track of how many states—and electoral votes—their candidate had won. And in this election, as never before, the electoral college would play a

prominent role in deciding who would become the next president of the United States.

Too Close to Call

By 10 P.M. on election night, the networks were beginning to change their minds about Florida. The election there was still too close to call, they said. They took Florida away from Gore and his vice presidential running mate, Senator Joseph Lieberman. As many Americans were going to bed, there was still no winner.

Early on Wednesday morning, around 2 A.M. on the East Coast, the networks finally declared that Bush and his running mate, Dick Cheney, had won Florida and the White House. Gore called Bush to **concede** the election. Then Gore headed for War Memorial Plaza in Nashville, Tennessee, where he planned to address his supporters. But as Gore and his staff were riding to the memorial, an aide suddenly got a message on his pager to call campaign headquarters. The situation had changed. Florida might not belong to Bush. His

Neither George W. Bush nor Al Gore could be declared the winner on Election Day. With the results unclear, Bush (right) and his running mate, Dick Cheney (left), began strategizing with campaign staff and legal advisors.

lead had shrunk to only about 500 popular votes. Florida law requires an automatic recount in close elections. The staff was told to keep Gore from giving his concession speech. From a room beneath the memorial, Gore called Bush again to explain that the situation had changed once more. He wasn't going to concede after all.

The 2000 election was not over yet. Gore was ahead in the popular and the electoral vote, but he didn't have an absolute majority in the electoral college. By the time Americans woke up on Wednesday morning, Bush was ahead by 1,784 popular votes in Florida, and he was also within striking distance of an electoral college win. Whichever man won Florida and its 25 electoral votes would win the election. But it would take more than a month to settle the results of what many people were calling the most astounding election in American history.

The Battle for Florida

Many problems surfaced with the election, but the **ballots** themselves became the main issue. Some officials thought the computer count of the punch-card ballots was inaccurate. And in Palm Beach County, some voters were confused about which punch hole on the ballot belonged to which candidate. Many of the county's residents began to wonder whether their vote had counted for their intended candidate. Protesters took to the streets to demand a new election. At the same time, Florida officials began to recount many of the state's ballots amid much controversy, as well as lawsuits from the Democrats and the Republicans.

A new word entered America's vocabulary: *chad,* the tiny piece of paper that a voter punches from a ballot. Different election boards used different standards or guidelines to count votes. Should a vote count if the chad was still hanging by two corners? What if the chad was merely indented? Florida's election boards debated these questions.

On Sunday, November 26, Florida's Secretary of State Katherine Harris, a Republican, declared that Bush was the winner by 537 votes. Democrats accused her of trying to help Bush win the election. On the same day that Harris certified Bush as the winner, his brother, Governor Jeb Bush, signed a Certificate of Ascertainment and sent the results to Washington. As part of the electoral process, every governor must sign this certificate, which lists the slates of electors and tells how many popular votes each candidate received. Certificates weren't due until December 12, and only two other governors had submitted them at this point. Democrats criticized Jeb Bush for rushing the results to Washington.

Florida Secretary of State Katherine Harris signs documents certifying that the state's 25 electoral votes belonged to George W. Bush. Under criticism from Democrats, Republican Governor Jeb Bush (right) sent the official results to Washington, D.C.

But this wasn't the end of the election. Gore refused to concede, and the next day he filed a lawsuit contesting the certification of the vote and asking for another recount. Meanwhile, Republicans in the state legislature had been looking into calling a special session to name their own slate of electors. A federal law passed after the controversial election of 1876 allows state legislatures to do this if the results are still unsettled after an election. Because the Republicans controlled the legislature, it was expected that they would name Republican electors. On December 12, Florida's House of Representatives voted for a Republican slate. The state Senate was scheduled to vote the next day.

The U.S. Supreme Court Rules

Throughout this election crisis, the news media was full of speculation about what might happen. What if Florida wound up with two sets of electors, one Republican and one Democratic? It had happened before in the election of 1876. Would this election end up being decided by the House of Representatives? That had happened before, too. There was even talk that the U.S. Supreme Court might get involved.

To the surprise of many, the court did agree to hear the case of *Bush v. Gore*. On December 12, the Supreme Court issued a complicated ruling. The way the counties in Florida were conducting recounts was unfair, the court said. There was no standard for what counted as a vote. The state did not have time to determine standards and start the recounts again. Therefore, the recounts must stop or Florida would miss the December 12 deadline for naming electors. With the recounts halted, Florida's 25 electoral votes went to Bush. The decision was controversial, even on the court itself. Four of the nine justices had voted against the decision.

Declaring a Winner

On December 18, the electors met in their state capitals to cast their votes. One elector from Washington, D.C., abstained, or did not vote. Gore had beaten Bush by more than half a million votes in the popular election. But the final

In his role as president of the Senate, Vice President Al Gore (left) was charged with reading the final results of the 2000 electoral vote.

tally in the electoral college was 271 votes for Bush and 266 votes for Gore.

These electoral votes became official on January 6, 2001, when they were opened and announced by the president of the Senate before a joint session of Congress. The president of the Senate also has the title of vice president of the United States. So it was Vice President Al Gore who announced that George W. Bush was the winner and next president of the United States.

Led by George Washington, America's founding fathers spent the summer of 1787 debating how the new nation's government would operate. The end result was the U.S. Constitution, which included an electoral system for selecting the president.

CHAPTER

2

Creating the Electoral College

SUMMERS IN PHILADELPHIA can be hot and unbearably humid. That is as true today as it was during the summer of 1787, when a group of delegates met at the Pennsylvania State House. Here they would write the Constitution, the document that would become the basis of the U.S. government. It didn't help that the **delegates** decided to keep the windows closed to prevent people from overhearing their debates. No one could control the weather, but the city did try to keep quiet. Gravel was spread along Chestnut Street to reduce the noise of horses and carriages passing by the building.

Delegates came to this Constitutional Convention from 12 of the 13 states. Only Rhode Island, whose politicians were opposed to creating a strong central government, refused to send delegates. Two future presidents, George Washington and James Madison, attended the sessions as delegates from Virginia. Washington was quickly elected president

James Madison became known as the Father of the Constitution. But he protested this title, saying the document was not "the offspring of a single brain" but rather "the work of many heads and many hands."

of the convention. Madison took a seat at the front of the room and recorded almost every word that was said.

The delegates did not set out to write a new Constitution. Instead, Congress had called this special convention to **amend** the Articles of Confederation, which loosely bound the states together. But some delegates soon realized that they needed to do more than just patch up that document. Under the Articles, the United States had difficulty collecting taxes from its citizens, raising an army, or conducting trade. The country did not have a president to lead the new country or a Supreme Court that would protect citizens' rights and interpret laws.

Today we take for granted that a president will be elected every four years. But when the Constitutional Convention opened in May 1787, the delegates weren't sure what type of leader they wanted in the office they called the *executive*. Should there be only one executive or a committee? How long should the term of office be? Alexander Hamilton, representing New York, was in favor of a long term. Otherwise, he said, we would have many ex-presidents wandering the country like ghosts. Maybe the executive should be appointed for life. But that sounded like the reign of a king, and Americans had just won their independence from the British king during the Revolutionary War (1775–1783).

Debates over Congress

At the same time they were debating the presidency, the delegates were trying to decide some important questions about Congress. Should it have one house or two? How should the states be represented? In 1787, Congress was made up of one house, and each state had one vote. States with large populations at that time, such as Virginia and Massachusetts, thought they should have more representatives. States with smaller populations, such as New Jersey and Delaware, did not like the idea of having less voting power than more populous states. And then there was the question of slaves. If representation in Congress were based on population, how should slaves be counted? States with large numbers of slaves would have an advantage. How the delegates finally answered these questions would eventually play a role in the setup of the electoral college.

Delegates from Virginia and New Jersey presented two conflicting plans to the convention. Under the Virginia plan, there would be one executive. Congress would have two houses, with each state's representation based on its population or wealth. Under the New Jersey plan, there would be a group of executives. Congress would have one house, with each state having an equal vote.

The two plans were fiercely debated. At one point, Delaware's Gunning Bedford, dripping with sweat, shouted at the representatives of the large states, "I do not, gentlemen, trust you." Then he threatened that if the small states didn't get what they wanted, they might abandon the United States and join up with a foreign power.

Some delegates feared the convention would break apart before they could reach any agreements. But finally, in mid-July, the convention began to resolve some of the issues. Under the Connecticut Plan, also known as the Great Compromise, there was something for everyone. Congress would have two houses—the Senate and the House of Representatives. Every state would have two senators, which

In what many historians consider a compromise of shame, the Founding Fathers agreed to count each slave as three-fifths of a person when determining a state's population for representation.

pleased the states with small populations. But in the House of Representatives, the number of members from each state would be based on the state's population. This plan pleased the more populous states. The delegates also decided that a slave would be counted as three-fifths of a person. They had not, however, resolved how to elect a president.

The Many Ways to Elect a President

Every presidential election system that delegates proposed seemed to have some flaw. They would vote in favor of one system and then change their minds. In fact, they needed 60 ballots to determine a method for selecting a president.

The delegates considered several options. Congress could choose the president. The problem they saw with this plan was that the president might feel he owed his job to Congress. The delegates feared that the president would then be more likely to do what Congress wanted, rather than act independently.

The state legislatures could choose the president. Under this plan, the president might feel he owed his job to the states. The delegates knew that a strong **federal** government was one of the key ideas in the Constitution. A system that would give too much power to the states would not be acceptable.

The people could choose the president. But the delegates feared that people would vote only for favorite sons, the candidates they knew from their own region of the country. This fear was real. The idea of a presidential candidate leaving home and traveling around the country to campaign was far in the future. Roads were poor. Communication was no better. The only ways to get a political message out were through letters or newspapers. At that time, it was just as difficult and time-consuming to travel over land from state to state, as it was to travel by boat to Europe.

Then there was Pennsylvania delegate James Wilson's idea. He suggested a lottery to choose electors. Balls would be put into a jar in Congress. A few of the balls would be colored gold. Every member of Congress would draw a ball. Those who drew gold balls would be the electors who chose the president. The system that the delegates finally agreed on included Wilson's idea of using electors to select the president.

An Electoral System

By early September, the delegates had reached a compromise between the legislature electing the president and a popular election. A group of electors would choose the president. Under Article II of the Constitution, each state would be entitled to the same number of electors as it had representatives and senators in Congress. Because every state had at least one representative and two senators, this plan ensured that all states would have at least three electors.

The Constitution left it up to the state legislatures to decide how electors would be chosen. The delegates thought the electors should be intelligent men who knew something about politics and national affairs, and who wrote to other people about these subjects. But they decided there were some people who shouldn't be electors. In the Constitution, they named senators, representatives, and other federal job holders as people who could not serve in this role.

The electors would meet not in one central place, but in their own states. This scattering of electors would make it more difficult for one of them to try to influence the others. Each elector would cast two votes. To keep electors from voting only for a favorite son, the founding fathers required them to cast one of their votes for a candidate who lived outside their own state. The votes would be sealed, sent to the president of the Senate, and then opened and counted in front of Congress. The person who received the most electoral votes would become the president—as long as this candidate received an absolute majority of the votes. If no one had an absolute majority, the election would be decided in the House of Representatives among the top five candidates. Each state would have one vote. Whether the electoral college or the House of Representatives decided the election, the second-place finisher would become the vice president. If there were a tie for vice president, the Senate would choose the winner.

The convention delegates thought the electoral college would probably serve as a nominating committee. In other words, it would narrow down the field of candidates to a few people. Then the final election would take place in the House. George Mason, a delegate from Virginia, predicted that 19 out of every 20 elections would be settled in the House. He was wrong. Only two elections, those of 1800 and 1824, have ever been decided in this manner.

The Constitution Is Ratified

Writing the Constitution was only the first step in establishing it as law. After the delegates signed it on September 17, 1787, it had to be sent to the states to be ratified, or approved. Nine of the 13 states needed to ratify the Constitution for it to take effect. Delegates Alexander Hamilton and James Madison, along with John Jay, the U.S. secretary of foreign affairs, wrote a series of newspaper essays called *The Federalist Papers.* These writings were meant to explain and promote the Constitution to the people of New York and were published in other states as well. In one essay, Hamilton described the process for choosing the president and said, "I . . . hesitate not to affirm that if the manner of it be not perfect, it is at least excellent."

Three months after Hamilton's essay was published, nine states ratified the Constitution and it went into effect on June 21, 1788. The founding fathers had drawn up the rules for electing the president. But how would these rules work under the test of a real election? Would the system prove to be as excellent as Hamilton predicted?

Thirty-nine delegates signed the Constitution. Although the word "elector" is in the Constitution, the term "electoral college" was not widely used until the 19th century.

General George Washington led the American colonies to victory during the Revolutionary War (1775–1783). Electors unanimously selected him as the first president of the United States.

CHAPTER **3**

Early Elections

THE DELEGATES TO the Constitutional Convention may have had a hard time agreeing on how the president should be elected, but there was one thing they all knew: No matter which system they chose, George Washington, the hero of the Revolutionary War, would be the first president of the United States. They did not know, however, who would be the vice president. Because Washington was a military man from the South, some delegates thought the vice president should be a civilian from the North. John Adams, who had played a key role in creating the Declaration of Independence, had recently returned to Boston from his post as minister to Great Britain. He wanted to run for office and soon decided he liked the idea of being vice president.

There were other candidates for vice president, but as the autumn of 1788 wore on, Adams was clearly the most popular. In fact, Adams became so popular that some of Washington's supporters began to worry. They had noticed a flaw in the electoral system. Electors did not vote separately for president and vice president. They cast two votes each, and the person who received the most votes and an absolute majority became president. The second-place finisher became vice president. If Adams received more votes than Washington, he could be elected president.

Washington's supporters got busy. Alexander Hamilton persuaded some electors to vote for candidates other than Adams. When the electoral votes were counted, Washington had received 69 votes from 69 electors. Adams received 34 votes, with the remaining 35 votes spread among 10 candidates. Adams, who was not aware of Hamilton's scheme, was surprised and upset that he had received so few votes. He threatened not to accept the vice presidency. But when the official messenger came with the news, he was packed and ready to go to New York City for the inauguration.

Voting in the Early Elections

The first presidential election took place fairly quickly. In autumn of 1788, Congress declared that the states must choose their electors by the first Wednesday in January 1789. The electors would vote on the first Wednesday in February. Only 10 of the 13 states participated. North Carolina and Rhode Island had not ratified the Constitution and were not yet part of the United States. In New York, the state legislature couldn't agree on a slate of electors by the January deadline and therefore could not participate in the election. The 10 states that did take part in the election used several different methods for choosing their electors. Three states used a direct popular election, with the voters choosing the electors. In five states, the legislatures chose the electors. Two states used a combination of popular election and election by the legislature.

It was up to each state to decide who could vote in a popular election. In most states, only white men over age 21 were eligible. They were often required to own property or pay taxes. It wasn't until the mid-1800s that white men who didn't own property were eligible to vote. And in 1870, all

men over age 21, regardless of
their race, had the right to vote.
Women did not win the right to
vote until 50 years later, in 1920.

In the early elections, some
states gave all their electoral votes
to the candidate who won the
statewide popular vote. Others
broke the state into voting districts.
Under that system, a state's electoral votes could be divided among
the candidates. If the state legislature chose the electors, the houses
might vote together or separately.
In some states, the legislature chose
the final slate of electors after a vote
by the people. In other states, the
legislature chose the electors only
if they hadn't received a majority

of the popular vote. States sometimes changed their systems
from election to election.

Today all voters go to the **polls** on the same day to elect
the president. Election Day is the first Tuesday after the first
Monday in November. But from 1792 to 1845, states could
set their own election days as long as they met one requirement: Electors had to be chosen sometime during the 34 days
before the first Wednesday in December, the day the electors
voted for president. Under this system, states tried to be among
the last to choose electors. In this way, they could see how
other states had voted before casting their own votes.

*George Washington's
1789 inauguration
took place at Federal
Hall in New York
City. In his inaugural
address, Washington
expressed his deter-
mination to make
America's model
of government
a success.*

The Birth of Political Parties

In 1792, Washington and Adams were easily reelected.
Once again, the electors cast their votes unanimously for
Washington. He had not been eager to run for a second term,
so it wasn't surprising when he chose not to seek a third term
in 1796. In his Farewell Address, he warned of the dangers

of political parties, organized groups that promote their ideas about government policies.

But Washington was too late. Men within his administration already had different ideas about the way the government should be run. Led by Alexander Hamilton, who had served as Washington's secretary of the treasury, the Federalist Party favored a strong central government. Their support for a national bank appealed to the merchants of New England and New York. They also wanted closer ties with Great Britain. Thomas Jefferson, once the secretary of state under Washington, led the Democratic-Republicans. Members of this party wanted the states to have more control. They envisioned a smaller role for the federal government, a view that appealed to farmers. The Democratic-Republicans thought that France, which was undergoing its own revolution, would be a better ally than Great Britain.

The election of 1796 was the first to involve political parties. And it was the only one in which the electors chose a president and vice president from different parties. Adams, the Federalist candidate for president, won the election with 71 electoral votes. Thomas Jefferson, the Democratic-Republican candidate for president, received 68 electoral votes and became vice president. Because electors did not vote separately for the two offices, a presidential candidate became vice president. This flaw in the Constitution would cause even more problems in the next election.

1800: Battle in the House

Adams and Jefferson had been friends before the 1796 election, and they still respected each other at the start of their term in office. But right from the beginning of their administration, the fact that they now represented different parties was too much for them to overcome. Adams soon stopped asking Jefferson for advice, and the two men faced off once again in the election of 1800.

The electors who cast their ballots in the 1800 election were no longer the independent men the founding fathers had

envisioned. When they ran as electors, they pledged to vote for one party's candidates. Their electoral votes were scheduled to be opened in the nation's new capital of Washington, D.C., on February 11, 1801. But even before that date, people were aware that something unusual was happening. The Federalist-controlled House might decide this election. Adams appeared to be out of the race, and it looked as if the vote would be very close between Jefferson and his vice-presidential running mate, Aaron Burr. In December, Alexander Hamilton began writing to Federalist members of Congress, urging them to vote for Jefferson if the election went to the House. Hamilton didn't like either Jefferson or Burr, but he viewed Jefferson as the lesser of two evils.

It was a snowy day when Congress met to open and count the electoral votes. Only one representative was absent. Another congressman, who was sick, was so determined to vote that he had himself carried into the House on his bed. As president of the Senate, Jefferson opened the electoral certificates from each state. The results were startling: Jefferson and Burr had tied with 73 votes each. The Federalists were out of the race. Adams had finished in third place

Elected in 1796, President John Adams (left) and Vice President Thomas Jefferson (right) became bitter enemies. They ran against each other again in the 1800 presidential election. Jefferson was the victor in that race.

with 65 votes, and his vice presidential candidate, Charles C. Pinckney, was in fourth place with 64 votes.

The Constitution said that if there were a tie between candidates, the members of the House would decide between them. Each state would have one vote, and the winner would need an absolute majority. With 16 states, that meant the winner would need to get at least nine votes. The members of the House began voting immediately. On the first ballot, Jefferson received eight votes, just one short of victory. Burr received six votes. The representatives of two states, Maryland and Vermont, were equally divided between the two candidates, so their votes did not count.

The House took another ballot and another and another. By midnight, they had voted 19 times, and there was still no winner. They continued the balloting through the night. One eyewitness said, "Many [congressmen] sent home for night caps and pillows, and wrapped in shawls and great-coats, lay about the floor of the committee rooms or sat sleeping in their seats. At one, two, and half-past two, the tellers roused the members from their slumbers, and took the same ballot as before." Why Burr, as the vice presidential candidate, didn't step aside for Jefferson is one of history's mysteries.

The voting continued for a week. Finally on February 17, after some behind-the-scenes negotiating, the votes shifted. On the 36th ballot, Jefferson won the presidency with 10 votes. With four votes, Burr became the vice president. On March 4, Jefferson walked from his rooms at a boarding house to the U.S. Capitol for his inauguration. He had done more than defeat Burr. By defeating Adams, Jefferson became the first candidate from one party to unseat a U.S. president belonging to another party.

Changing the Constitution

After the election of 1800, it was clear that something needed to be done about the way the vice president was chosen. The only way to change the system was to amend the Constitution. The 12th Amendment, ratified in September

Federalist Alexander Hamilton and Democratic-Republican Aaron Burr often clashed politically. But when Hamilton insulted Burr, their battle became personal and ended in a pistol duel. Burr killed Hamilton and was charged with murder.

1804, said electors would now vote separately for president and vice president. The candidate for president who had a majority of votes would be the winner. If no one had a majority, the House would choose the president from among the top three candidates. Each state would have one vote. The candidate for vice president who won the majority of votes would win that election. If no vice presidential candidate had a majority, the Senate would choose a winner from the top two candidates. In this case, each senator would have one vote.

What became of the men involved in the election of 1800? Thomas Jefferson ran for president again in 1804. This time he ran with a different vice president. He and other members of his party had decided Aaron Burr couldn't be trusted. In later years, Jefferson and his former opponent, Adams, began writing letters and became friends again. They died within hours of each other on July 4, 1826, the 50th anniversary of the Declaration of Independence, which they had created together.

Hamilton and Burr did not become friends. In 1804, knowing that he wasn't going to be Jefferson's running mate, Burr decided to run for governor of New York. When he lost the election in the spring, he was sure Hamilton had something to do with it. Then he read in the newspaper that Hamilton had insulted him. In July 1804, he killed Hamilton in a duel.

When the 1824 presidential election went to the House of Representatives to decide, John Quincy Adams came out the winner. After his term as president, he served in the House until his death in 1848.

CHAPTER 4

Political Maneuvers and Scandals

WHEN JOHN ADAMS lost the election of 1800, his son was in Berlin. John Quincy Adams was serving as the U.S. minister to Prussia. President Adams didn't want to give Thomas Jefferson the satisfaction of replacing his son with another minister. In one of his last acts in office, he signed the papers ordering John Quincy Adams to come home. But the younger Adams did not want to return to America. In Europe, he could spend his days reading and writing. In Boston, he would probably have to go back to practicing law, a job he hated. His father warned John Quincy to stay away from politics. "If I were to go over my life again, I would be a shoemaker rather than an American statesman," the former president said bitterly.

John Quincy Adams did take up law again, and despite his father's warning, it wasn't long before he turned to politics. In April 1802, less than a year after he returned home, he was elected to the Massachusetts State Senate. In 1803 he moved on to the U.S. Senate. But his days as a foreign minister were not over. During President James Madison's administration (1809–1817), he served first as minister to Russia and then to Great Britain.

When James Monroe became president in 1817, he chose Adams as his secretary of state, the member of the president's cabinet who handles relations with foreign governments. Adams knew that three former secretaries of state—Jefferson, Madison, and Monroe—had gone on to become president. By December 1823, he had decided to try for the presidency himself. With his wife, Louisa, Adams began planning a ball for January. The guest of honor would be a man named Andrew Jackson.

Jackson was a popular figure from Tennessee, who had briefly served in both the U.S. House and Senate in the 1790s. He was best known as the hero of the War of 1812 (1812–1814) who had defeated the British in the Battle of New Orleans. During the First Seminole War (1817–1818), he gained additional fame for his military attacks against the American Indians and the Spanish in Florida. In 1821, President Monroe made Jackson governor of the new Florida Territory. Jackson's actions in Florida helped to make him even more popular, especially in what were then the western states. The Tennessee legislature nominated Jackson for president in 1822, a full two years before the next election. He needed more time in the national spotlight, so a year later, the legislature made him a U.S. Senator again. Jackson arrived in Washington in early December 1823. A little more than a month later, on January 8, he was at the Adams house, attending the ball in his honor.

The purpose of the ball was to celebrate the anniversary of the Battle of New Orleans. But Adams had another motive. He knew that Jackson would be a strong contender for president. If Adams was going to win, he needed Jackson on his **ticket** to bring in votes from the western states. On the night of the ball, a thousand people crowded into the Adams home. Louisa Adams took Jackson's arm and walked from room to room, introducing the new senator. To many guests, an Adams-Jackson ticket seemed likely. But Jackson wanted to be president, not Adams's vice president.

1824: The House Decides

Today a series of **primary elections** and **caucuses** helps political parties determine who will be their candidates. Any eligible voter can vote in a primary or attend a caucus meeting. This process was much different in the early 19th century, when a group of congressmen from each party chose the candidates in secret caucuses. The Democratic-Republicans called a caucus for February 1824. Some Democratic-Republicans objected to the caucus system because it was secretive and didn't give the people a chance to be involved. Few members of Congress attended the caucus, which nominated William H. Crawford, then the secretary of the treasury. Adams and Jackson paid no attention to the caucus results. Neither did statesman Henry Clay, who was also running for president.

In 1824, John Quincy Adams (far right) and his wife, Louisa, hosted a ball to honor war hero Andrew Jackson (center). Adams hoped Jackson would run as his vice president.

One advantage of the caucus system was that it narrowed the field of candidates. Now with four candidates, it seemed likely that no one would receive enough electoral votes to win an absolute majority. Henry Clay was counting on the election going to the House of Representatives. As **Speaker of the House,** he could drum up enough votes to make himself president. What he hadn't counted on was finishing fourth in the electoral college.

In 1824, only six of the 24 states were still using their legislatures to choose electors. The rest used the popular vote. More men were eligible to vote in this election because, by this point, most states no longer required voters to own property. For the first time, a national total for the popular vote was recorded. Jackson was the winner with 152,901 votes. Adams came in second with 114,023 votes. Crawford and Clay each had about 47,000 votes. But the election was not over yet.

In the electoral college, Jackson received 99 votes, Adams 84, Crawford 41, and Clay 37. Although Jackson had won the most votes, he needed 32 more to have an absolute majority. Therefore, the members of the House would decide the election. Under the 12th amendment, the House would choose from among the top three finishers. Clay might have wished the Constitution had never been changed. Under the original plan, the House chose from among the top five finishers. Now Clay would have to use his power to make another man president.

On January 9, 1825, Adams wrote in his diary: "Mr. Clay came at six, and spent the evening with me in a long conversation explanatory of the past and prospective of the future." Clay had won the electoral votes of three western states—Kentucky, Missouri, and Ohio. He promised those votes to Adams.

The House was scheduled to vote on February 9, 1825. Jackson was in bed, recovering from a fall. Most people expected the House would take days to settle the election as it did in 1800. Most people also knew the New York delegation was divided over which candidate should get its support. As the New York members prepared to vote, congressman Stephen Van Rensselaer remained undecided. He closed his eyes in prayer. When he opened them, he saw an Adams ballot at his feet. Taking that as a sign from God, he picked it up and put it in the New York ballot box. Adams now had enough ballots in his favor for the New York delegation to give him its vote.

According to the Constitution, members of the House voted by state. Each state had one vote. The presidential winner needed votes from at least 13 states to have a majority of the 24 states. It took only one ballot for Adams to win the election. He received 13 votes to Jackson's seven and Crawford's four. On that day, Jackson became the first man to win the popular vote but lose the White House.

Soon after he won the election, Adams announced that Henry Clay would be his secretary of state. Jackson was outraged and accused Adams of giving Clay the job as a reward for securing Adams's election to the presidency. "Was there ever witnessed such a bare faced-corruption in any country before?" he shouted. Voters in the western states were angry too. They felt that Clay had bargained their votes for the cabinet post. Jackson's supporters took up the cry of "corrupt bargain."

The Next Elections

Although the election was four years away, the 1828 campaign for the White House began immediately. It was one of the nastiest campaigns in American history. Adams had been a respected and effective secretary of state, but he was able to accomplish little as president. Congress worked against him, and the "corrupt bargain" charge followed him everywhere.

By 1828, four more states had changed their laws to allow voters, instead of the legislature, to choose the slate of electors in a popular election. Now only two states—South Carolina and Delaware—were using the legislature system. Jackson won both the popular vote and the electoral vote in 1828. In the electoral college, he received 178 votes to Adams's 83 votes. Jackson's win was proclaimed a victory for the common man and the western states.

Andrew Jackson won the 1828 election by a large margin in the electoral college. After his inauguration, well-wishers mobbed the White House.

Adams did not attend Jackson's inauguration. The two men were bitter enemies. To this day, only one other president has not attended his successor's inauguration. That man was John Adams. Like his father, John Quincy Adams left the White House and went back to Massachusetts. But unlike his father, he later returned to Washington as a congressman.

Jackson went on to win reelection in 1832. Four years later, in 1836, his vice president, Martin Van Buren, won the presidential election. Although Van Buren won a majority in the electoral college, his vice presidential running mate, Richard Mentor Johnson, did not. A group of electors refused to vote for Johnson because he was living with a woman of African-American descent, and they had two children. As the Constitution required, the election went to the Senate, where Johnson received enough votes to win. This case was the only time that the Senate has been called upon to decide a vice presidential election.

Campaign banners proclaim the 1876 candidates for president and vice president. Democrats Samuel J. Tilden and Thomas A. Hendricks battled the Republican ticket of Rutherford B. Hayes and William A. Wheeler.

CHAPTER **5**

The Elections of 1876 and 1888

BY THE MID-1800s, two parties dominated politics in the United States—the Democrats and the Republicans. In the election of 1876, Republican Rutherford B. Hayes squared off against Democrat Samuel J. Tilden. Hayes was a former congressman and governor of Ohio. Tilden was governor of New York and was best known for breaking up the Tweed Ring, a group of politicians who stole millions of dollars through New York City improvement schemes. In reality, there was little difference between the two candidates. With Hayes and Tilden, both political parties offered reform candidates who pledged to clean up the government. The current president, Ulysses S. Grant, had spent two terms in the White House that were marked by scandal and corruption.

Both candidates also pledged to remove the last federal troops from the South. After the Civil War ended in 1865, the Radical Republicans, a faction of the anti-slavery Republican Party, favored harsh punishment for the former Confederate States. They followed a plan of Reconstruction that consisted of depriving some whites, including former Confederate soldiers, of their right to vote and giving this right to former slaves. Southern African American voters helped elect Republicans in state and local government. The Republicans replaced Democrats who had long had a stronghold in the South. But as whites regained the right to vote and used fraud and violence to keep African Americans from voting, Democratic governments gradually came back into power in the South. By 1876, there were only three states where Republicans still controlled the government with the backing of federal troops. These states were Florida, Louisiana, and South Carolina, and they would play a crucial role in the presidential election of 1876.

On the morning after the election, it appeared that Tilden would be the winner. All the results were not yet in, but at that point Hayes had 166 electoral votes and Tilden had 184 votes, just one short of the number he needed to win. Still unclaimed were 19 electoral votes from Florida, Louisiana, and South Carolina, and it looked as if Tilden would win at least two of those states. But Republican Party officials were busy doing their own math. They realized that if Hayes could capture all 19 of those votes, he would have 185 votes and the presidency. They decided simply to declare that he was the winner in those states.

On December 6, the electors voted in their state capitals. In Florida, Louisiana, and South Carolina, Republican electors voted for Hayes. But Democratic state officials hadn't given up. They certified that Tilden had won all of those electoral votes. In each of the three states, there were now two sets of electoral returns, one Republican and one Democratic. Which one should count as the official set?

Each side accused the other of fraud. The Republicans accused the Democrats of using intimidation to keep African American voters away from the polls. The Democrats accused the Republicans of destroying Tilden ballots by dumping them or covering them with ink. There were rumors that Southerners were ready to fight another civil war if Hayes was elected. At the Hayes home in Ohio, a bullet came flying through a window while the family was eating dinner.

Meanwhile out in Oregon, another strange situation had developed. Originally, it appeared that all three of the state's electoral votes would go to Hayes, the Republican candidate. But then it was revealed that one of the Republican electors was a postmaster, a federal job. According to the Constitution, he could not be an elector. To take his place, the governor appointed the elector who had received the next highest number of votes. That man was a Democrat. But the postmaster, perhaps realizing that every vote counted in this election, resigned his job so he could serve as an elector. As a result, Oregon also sent two sets of electoral returns to Washington, D.C. One gave all three votes to Hayes. The other gave two votes to Hayes and one to Tilden.

The Electoral Commission of 1877

The Constitution did not say who should count the votes after they reached Congress. The Democrats had a majority in the house, while the Republicans controlled the Senate. The body that counted the votes would be sure to count the electoral return that was in the majority party's favor. To solve the vote-counting problem, Congress passed the Electoral Commission Bill on January 18, 1877. The commission would decide which set of electoral votes was valid in each of the four states. The commission would have 15 members—five from the Senate, five from the House, and five from the Supreme Court. The Senate

After four states each submitted two sets of electoral votes, Congress created a 15-member Electoral Commission to decide the 1876 election.

would choose three Republicans and two Democrats, while the House would choose two Republicans and three Democrats. The bill appointed four Supreme Court justices to the commission, two Republicans and two Democrats, and the four justices were to choose a fifth. The justices were expected to pick David Davis, an independent. The commission would then have an equal number of Democrats and Republicans, plus one person who favored neither party.

A problem arose with this plan. On January 25, the Illinois state legislature chose Justice Davis as the state's new U.S. Senator. The four justices had to pick someone else for the commission. They chose Joseph P. Bradley, a Republican who was supposed to act impartially.

When it came time to vote, however, Bradley sided with the Republicans. The cases in all four states had the same result. The commission's vote was eight to seven in favor of the Hayes electors. For the election to be official, Congress had to accept the electoral votes that the commission had approved. Democrats started a delaying process called a **filibuster,** which was designed to postpone the final count. The Democratic members kept voting to recess, or stop working. Meanwhile, Inauguration Day was drawing closer, and there was still no **president-elect.**

In late February, Republicans met with Southern Democrats in Washington, D.C. They struck a deal. The Democrats agreed to accept the Electoral Commission's results, which meant Hayes would be the new president. In return, Republicans agreed to withdraw all federal troops from the South, bringing an end to Reconstruction. As part of the agreement, Hayes was to appoint a Southerner as postmaster general, a cabinet position that controlled many **patronage** jobs. Money would also go to the South for a transcontinental railroad and other internal improvements. Southerners would be allowed to run their own states and decide how the former slaves should be treated. This would eventually lead to segregation and other policies that denied African Americans their civil rights.

On Friday, March 2, Congress declared Hayes the winner, and he was sworn in the next day. Despite earlier predictions, another civil war did not break out. Tilden, who had won the popular vote, did not encourage his supporters to challenge the results. He said of the election, "I shall receive from posterity the credit of having been elected to the highest position in the gift of the people, without any of the cares and responsibilities of the office." After the election, Hayes became known as "Rutherfraud" and "His Fraudulency." In 1876, he promised to run for only one term. He kept his word and did not seek reelection in 1880.

As a result of this election, Congress passed the Electoral Count Act of 1887. This law gives responsibility to the states to resolve their own electoral disputes. But the law still allows Congress to challenge an electoral vote. When a vote is contested, each house in Congress meets to debate and vote on the issue. A majority of both houses must agree in order for an electoral vote to be discarded.

The Election of 1888

No special electoral commission was needed to straighten out the results of the election of 1888. Democrat Grover Cleveland was already sitting in the White House. His opponent for reelection was Republican Benjamin Harrison of Indiana. Harrison was the grandson of William Henry Harrison, the ninth president of the United States.

The biggest issue of this campaign was the tariff, a tax added to goods made in other countries. Big businesses traditionally favored high tariffs because they increased the price of foreign-made goods. As a result, people would be more likely to buy American products. Consumers favored low tariffs because they could choose from a wider selection of cheaper goods. President Cleveland sided with consumers, a position that upset business owners in the northern states. These business owners raised a great deal of money to campaign against Cleveland.

On Election Day, Cleveland won the popular vote by a very slim margin. Out of approximately 11 million votes, Cleveland received about 100,000 more than Harrison did. That's a difference of less than 1 percent. But in the electoral college, Harrison won the election with 233 votes. Cleveland trailed with 168 electoral votes. How did that happen? Looking back, historians can see that Cleveland won the popular election by large majorities in some states. In contrast, Harrison's majorities were smaller, but he managed to win more states. The issue that defeated Cleveland was the tariff. He needed to pick up votes in the

The tariff on imported goods was a major issue of the 1888 election. This anti-tariff political cartoon shows a man opening a "tariff protection" gate to let a waterfall of European goods through, thus flooding and destroying American manufacturers.

northern states, but his low-tariff ideas were not popular there. He did not even win in New York, his home state.

Perhaps the most remarkable fact about this election was the silence that greeted the results. Unlike the Adams-Jackson contest of 1824 or the Hayes-Tilden election of 1876, the public did not seem too upset by the outcome. Cleveland and Harrison met again in the election of 1892. This time Cleveland won both the popular and the electoral vote. He remains the only president to serve two terms interrupted by the presidency of another man.

Americans go to the polls every four years to cast ballots in the presidential election. They vote for electors who have pledged their votes to certain candidates.

6

The Electoral College Today

EVERY FOUR YEARS, Americans go to the polls to vote for a president and vice president. In most states, voters see only the names of the candidates on the ballot. The words *electors for* are often written above the candidates' names, the only clue that voters are really choosing electors on Election Day. A few states use the long ballot, which actually lists all the names of the electors.

The political parties in most states choose their own slates of electors. Serving as an elector is often a reward for large donations of money or for years of service to the party. The Constitution states that electors cannot be members of Congress or hold a federal job. The 14th Amendment to the Constitution, passed after the Civil War, also prohibits anyone who was involved in a rebellion against the United States, or who has helped enemies of the country, from serving as an elector.

Each state has the same number of electors as it has senators and representatives in Congress. That number can change over time as a state's population grows or shrinks. For example, Virginia now has less than 3 percent of all electoral votes. But back in the 1790s, it had more power in the electoral college, with 15 percent of the electors. A new national census is taken every 10 years and is used to determine how many representatives each state has in Congress. In the 2000 election, Florida had 25 electors because it had 23 representatives and two senators. These numbers were based on the 1990 census. The most recent census, taken in 2000, showed that Florida's population had grown. For the 2004 and 2008 elections, the state will have 27 electors because it will have 25 representatives and two senators.

Washington, D.C., is also entitled to participate in the electoral college. When the 23rd Amendment to the Constitution was passed in 1961, the nation's capital was given the same number of electors as the state with the smallest population. For 2004 and 2008, that number stands at three electors. The total number of electors is 538, based on 100 senators plus 435 representatives plus three electors for Washington, D.C. To win the presidency, a candidate must receive a majority, or at least 270 votes.

Today the people in every state and in Washington, D.C., choose which slate of electors will cast votes in the electoral college. In all but two states, the candidate who wins the popular vote receives all of that state's electoral votes. The Constitution does not require this "winner-take-all" system. Instead, it is a method that the states adopted over the years. Maine and Nebraska are the only states where it is possible to divide electoral votes among candidates. But so far, both states have given all their votes to one candidate in each election.

The Electoral College Meets

Before the electors meet, each governor must submit a Certificate of Ascertainment to the Archivist of the United States in Washington, D.C. The certificate lists the slates of

Electors meet in their state capitals to cast their votes for a presidential ticket.

electors and how many votes each received. On the first Monday after the second Wednesday in December, the electors meet in their state capitals to cast their votes. They may be paid a small amount for their day of service. In Massachusetts, electors receive $3 a day plus $1 for every five miles they travel to the capital city of Boston. When it comes time to vote, electors cast separate ballots for president and vice president. The Constitution requires that one vote be for someone who is not from the elector's own state. In many states, electors give their votes aloud instead of using a written ballot.

Most of the time, electors vote for the candidate that they have pledged to support. In fact, only about 10 electors have been "faithless" and voted for another candidate. There is no federal law requiring electors to honor their pledges. However, 26 states plus Washington, D.C., bind their electors with a state law, a state pledge, or a party pledge. No one has ever been taken to court for being a faithless elector.

After the votes have been counted, the electors sign the official Certificate of Vote, which is sent to the president of the Senate. The next step takes place on January 6, when the House of Representatives and the Senate meet in a joint session. The House and Senate each appoint two **tellers.**

The president of the Senate, who is also the U.S. vice president, gives the results of the electoral college vote before a joint session of Congress.

Starting with Alabama and continuing through to Wyoming, the Certificates of Vote are then opened in alphabetical order by the president of the Senate, who hands them to the tellers for counting and recording. The president of the Senate, who is also the vice president of the United States, announces the name of the winner. This announcement ends the electoral process.

If no candidate has an absolute majority in the electoral college, however, the House of Representatives chooses a winner from among the top three vote getters. Each state has one vote, no matter how many representatives it has. For example, if the 2000 election decision had gone to the House, Vermont, with one representative, and California, with 54 representatives, would each have had only one vote. The representative from Washington, D.C., who doesn't have a vote in Congress, is not allowed to vote. To win, a candidate must receive an absolute majority, or at least 26 votes. To decide how they will cast their vote, the members of each state's congressional delegation hold an election. If that vote results in a tie, that state does not cast a vote.

If no vice presidential candidate receives a majority of votes in the electoral college, the Senate must decide between the top two candidates. In this case, each senator—not each state—gets one vote. To win, a candidate must receive an absolute majority, or at least 51 votes.

One Elector's Experience

What is it like to be an elector? Ken Jarin, a Philadelphia lawyer, is a longtime friend and supporter of Al Gore. In the 2000 election, Pennsylvania's Democratic electors were chosen by the state Democratic Party and the Gore campaign. Jarin knew on election night that his candidate had won the popular vote in Pennsylvania and that he would be an elector. He soon received his official notification from the governor.

Jarin and his family traveled to the state capital of Harrisburg for a day filled with speeches and ceremony. The electoral college met in the ornate House of Representatives chambers in the state capitol building on December 18, 2000. The electors were sworn in. Then they voted for president and vice president by writing their votes on paper ballots and dropping them in a wooden ballot box. After the votes were counted, two electors escorted the governor into the House chambers to hear the results. The governor made a speech, and the electors signed the Certificate of Vote. Then they moved on to the governor's mansion for lunch. For their services, the electors took home souvenir pens and the Bibles from their swearing-in ceremony.

Jarin said the day was exciting because rumors were swirling that some electors in other states might change their minds and vote for Gore. Only a few electors needed to switch their votes for Gore to become president. But in the end, the only surprise was that one Washington, D.C., elector decided not to cast a vote. She was protesting the fact that Washington, D.C.'s representative cannot vote in Congress. All other electors remained faithful to their political parties, and George W. Bush won the election.

California residents protest outside the state capitol as electors gather inside to cast their votes in the 2000 presidential election. Opponents of the electoral college believe it should be replaced with a national popular vote.

CHAPTER 7

Should the Electoral College System Change?

DURING THE SIX games of the 1996 World Series, the Atlanta Braves scored a total of 26 runs. The New York Yankees scored only 18 runs, but won the World Series anyway. Why? Because they won four games, and the Braves won only two. The Braves could argue that this outcome wasn't fair. But the rules say that the championship goes to the team that wins four games, not the team that scores the most runs. In a similar way, the winner of the presidential election is the person who receives the most electoral votes, not the one who wins the most popular votes. Those are the rules, but should the rules be changed? Even before the 2000 election, there were calls to get rid of the electoral college. In the past 200 years, Congress has seen more than 700 proposals for changing or abolishing the electoral college. More amendments have been proposed for that part of the Constitution than for any other section.

Arguments Against the Electoral College

Those who want to abolish the electoral college argue that it's an out-of-date system from a period in our history when only part of the population could vote. They say the system doesn't work the way the founding fathers intended because they had no idea that political parties and national campaigns would play major roles in presidential elections. The founding fathers didn't know that electors would pledge to vote for their party's candidates, and that states would adopt a winner-take-all method for awarding electoral votes.

The biggest problem, say some people, is that the popular-vote winner may lose in the electoral college, and thus lose the entire election. This situation has occurred four times in our history: the elections of 1824 (John Quincy Adams vs. Andrew Jackson), 1876 (Rutherford B. Hayes vs. Samuel J. Tilden), 1888 (Benjamin Harrison vs. Grover Cleveland), and most recently in 2000 (George W. Bush vs. Al Gore). And, with a slight shift in votes in key states, the outcome could have changed in more than 20 presidential elections. For example, in 1976, if Gerald Ford had won about 5,600 more votes in Ohio and about 3,700 more votes in Hawaii, he would have won those electoral votes and the election.

There are several other arguments against the electoral college system. In some states, people might not bother to vote because they think their votes don't count. For example, a Republican in a traditionally Democratic state might feel there is no point in voting because the state's electoral votes will go to the Democratic candidate. This attitude may lead to another issue: A state receives the same number of electoral votes, no matter how many people actually go to the polls.

The basis for determining each state's electoral votes is an issue as well, argue some people. The number of electoral votes is determined by the census, which is taken once every 10 years. For example, a state's population could have grown between 1990 and 2000, but that growth wouldn't be reflected in its electoral votes until the 2004 election.

Third-party candidate Ross Perot ran for president in 1992. Although he won nearly one-fifth of the popular vote across the country, he received no votes in the electoral college.

Therefore, the number of electoral votes a state has may not properly represent the number of voters. Another point is that campaigns themselves focus on the electoral college rather than on the voters. Candidates concentrate on the issues of states that have many electoral votes or states where it is not clear who will win.

The winner-take-all approach used by most states raises other concerns, say those opposed to the electoral college system. It may make a candidate's victory appear larger than it really is. The most outstanding example was Ronald Reagan's victory in the 1980 election. He won 50.7 percent of the popular vote, but an overwhelming 90.9 percent of the electoral vote. The winner-take-all system also makes it difficult for **third-party** candidates to do well. In the 1992 election, Ross Perot won 19 percent of the popular vote. But he didn't win any electoral votes because his popular votes were scattered across the country.

Opponents of the electoral college argue that it should be replaced by a national popular election. This direct election would ensure that the candidate chosen by the most voters would win the White House. One plan suggests that the victor must win at least 40 percent of the vote. If no candidate meets this requirement, there would be a runoff election between the two top finishers. Those in favor of this system say elections run in this manner on the state and local level work well. A popular election would also eliminate the fear that a group of faithless electors could decide to disregard the popular vote and vote for another candidate. After all, electors have done some strange things. In 1872, Democratic candidate Horace Greeley died between Election Day and the day the electors voted. Three electors voted for him anyway.

Arguments for the Electoral College

Those in favor of the electoral college point out that it has been working well for more than 200 years. They argue that only once did it directly deny someone the presidency, in the Harrison-Cleveland election of 1888. In 1876, it was not the electoral college, but the corrupt Electoral Commission that decided the election in favor of Hayes. In 1824, it was the House of Representatives that chose John Quincy Adams over Andrew Jackson. Also, we don't really know the complete popular vote for the 1824 election because in six states, the legislatures chose the electors. The results of the 2000 election are still being debated. But many of those who favor the electoral college system argue that it was the Supreme Court, and not the electoral college, that denied Al Gore the presidency.

Proponents of the electoral college say it forces presidential candidates to pay attention to small states and the special interests of groups such as farmers, minorities, and organized labor. Without it, candidates would ignore what is important in individual states and campaign strictly on issues that have broad national appeal. As the system stands, a candidate cannot win enough votes in the electoral college simply by appealing to one region of the country. That is why George Wallace's third-party bid for the

Proponents of the electoral system say it encourages candidates to address issues such as farming, which is important to many of the less populous states.

presidency failed in 1968. He captured 46 electoral votes, but his support was only in the South, and therefore he did not have enough votes to win the electoral college.

Some people are proponents of the electoral college because it supports the two-party system. Candidates compete in a series of primary elections and caucuses for each party's nomination. Candidates who do not receive the nomination simply drop out of the election. If there was a possibility of a popular vote runoff, these candidates might stay in the race, dividing the party votes among several candidates. It's likely that more third-party candidates would run, which might reduce the power of the two major parties. As it stands, the electoral college strengthens the two-party system.

A national popular election could result in more recounts, say those who favor the electoral college system. Right now, if the results are close in a state, that state's votes might be recounted. The 2000 election showed how messy that process could become. What if the entire country's votes had to be recounted? In 1960 John F. Kennedy defeated Richard Nixon by less than two-tenths of one percent in the popular vote. In such a close election, the electoral college acts as a tiebreaker. As for the fear of faithless electors, say proponents, there have only been about 10 in the entire history of the electoral college, and they have never affected the outcome of an election.

Room for Agreement

There is one point on which both sides agree. The Constitution says that if no candidate wins an absolute majority in the electoral college, the House of Representatives chooses the president from the top three candidates. Neither side is comfortable with this idea because there are no guidelines for how representatives should vote. They might vote along party lines, for the candidate that won in their district, for the popular vote winner, or for the candidate who is ahead in the electoral college. Representatives are free to choose the basis for their vote.

Both sides also have concerns about the power that the electoral college system gives to both small states and large states. As a bloc of voters, residents in large states with many electoral votes, such as California, New York, and Texas, have the advantage in the electoral college system. Their electoral votes hold great weight in determining who will win the presidency. Small states, on the other hand, have more power per citizen than states with larger populations. If the election goes into the House of Representatives, each state receives one vote, no matter how large its population. Because each state must have at least three electoral votes, the small states also have greater power in the electoral college as a whole. For example, North Dakota has a population of about 642,000 people and three electoral votes. There is one electoral vote for approximately every 214,000 people. In California, which has a population of almost 34 million people and 55 electoral votes, there is one electoral vote for about every 618,000 people.

Is this distribution of electoral votes a good thing? Yes, say those who argue that the electoral votes force politicians to pay attention to the small states. No, say those who think

George W. Bush took the oath of office during his inauguration in Washington, D.C. Many people believe that, like the inauguration, the electoral college is an American tradition.

it gives the small states too much power in relation to their populations. In 1787, the Constitutional Convention delegates spent a great deal of time arguing about how much power the small states should have. More than 200 years later, the argument continues.

The founding fathers did not intend to make it easy to change the system of government they had worked so hard to devise during that summer in 1787. Abolishing the electoral college would require an amendment to the Constitution. For the amendment to pass, two-thirds of both the House of Representatives and the Senate would need to vote in favor of it. Then the legislatures in three-fourths, or 38, of the states would also have to approve it. Passing an amendment is a long and difficult process. For now, the electoral college will continue to play a role in the way Americans elect their president.

Electoral College Votes by State for 2004 and 2008 Elections

State	Votes	State	Votes
Alabama	9	Nebraska	5
Alaska	3	Nevada	5
Arizona	10	New Hampshire	4
Arkansas	6	New Jersey	15
California	55	New Mexico	5
Colorado	9	New York	31
Connecticut	7	North Carolina	15
Delaware	3	North Dakota	3
District of Columbia	3	Ohio	20
Florida	27	Oklahoma	7
Georgia	15	Oregon	7
Hawaii	4	Pennsylvania	21
Idaho	4	Rhode Island	4
Illinois	21	South Carolina	8
Indiana	11	South Dakota	3
Iowa	7	Tennessee	11
Kansas	6	Texas	34
Kentucky	8	Utah	5
Louisiana	9	Vermont	3
Maine	4	Virginia	13
Maryland	10	Washington	11
Massachusetts	12	West Virginia	5
Michigan	17	Wisconsin	10
Minnesota	10	Wyoming	3
Mississippi	6	**TOTAL**	**538**
Missouri	11		
Montana	3	**VOTES NEEDED TO WIN**	**270**

Glossary

Absolute majority—At least one over half of the total.

Amend—To change or revise.

Ballot—A sheet of paper used to cast a secret vote.

Caucus—A meeting of a group of people belonging to the same political party to choose candidates or decide on a policy.

Concede—To acknowledge that another candidate has defeated you in an election.

Delegate—A representative at a convention or conference.

Electors—One of several representatives selected by a political party and chosen by a state's voters to elect the president and vice president; voters choose a slate, or list, of electors when they vote for a presidential ticket.

Federal—A central government that has authority over states and their governments.

Filibuster—Unlimited debate or delaying tactics to keep a bill or issue from being brought to a vote in the Senate or House.

Patronage—The right to appoint a person to a job in government.

Poll—A place where votes are cast.

Popular vote—The total vote cast by individual voters for candidates in an election.

President-elect—The person who has been elected president but has not yet taken the oath of office.

Primary election—An election in which voters nominate a party candidate for a political office.

Speaker of the House—The leader and most powerful member of the House of Representatives; the speaker is chosen by the party that has the most members in the House.

Teller—A person appointed by Congress to count electoral votes to determine the winner of an election.

Third party—Any political party that is not one of the two main parties, currently the Democrats and the Republicans.

Ticket—A list of candidates for an election, often divided among parties.

Further Reading

Best, Judith A. *The Choice of the People? Debating the Electoral College.* Lanham, Md.: Rowman & Littlefield Publishers, Inc., 1996.

Campbell, James E. *The American Campaign: U.S. Presidential Campaigns and the National Vote.* College Station, Texas: Texas A&M University Press, 2000.

Collier, Christopher. *Creating the Constitution: 1787.* The Drama of American History. New York: Benchmark Books, 1999.

Correspondents of the *New York Times. 36 Days: The Complete Chronicle of the 2000 Presidential Election Crisis.* New York: Henry Holt, 2001.

Gutman, Dan. *Landslide! A Kid's Guide to the U.S. Elections.* New York: Aladdin Paperbacks, 2000.

Longley, Lawrence D. and Neal R. Peirce. *The Electoral College Primer 2000.* New Haven, Conn.: Yale University Press, 1999.

Rakove, Jack N. *Original Meanings: Politics and Ideas in the Making of the Constitution.* New York: A.A. Knopf, 1996.

Robinson, Lloyd. *The Stolen Election: Hayes Versus Tilden, 1876.* New York: Tom Doherty Associates, 2001.

Weisberger, Bernard A. *America Afire: Jefferson, Adams, and the Revolutionary Election of 1800.* New York: William Morrow, 2000.

Web site

The National Archives and Records Administration's official electoral college Web site:
[http://www.nara.gov/fedreg/elctcoll/]

ABOUT THE AUTHOR: Martha S. Hewson is a freelance writer and editor who works on projects for children and adults. She is the author of *Stonewall Jackson* in the Chelsea House series FAMOUS FIGURES OF THE CIVIL WAR ERA. A former editor at *The Philadelphia Inquirer* and *McCall's* magazine, she has a bachelor's degree in American history and literature from Harvard University and a master's degree in journalism from Columbia University. She lives near Philadelphia.

SENIOR CONSULTING EDITOR: Arthur M. Schlesinger, Jr. is the leading American historian of our time. He won the Pulitzer Prize for his book *The Age of Jackson* (1945) and again for *A Thousand Days* (1965). This chronicle of the Kennedy Administration also won a National Book Award. Professor Schlesinger is the Albert Schweitzer Professor of the Humanities at the City University of New York and has been involved in several other Chelsea House projects, including the REVOLUTIONARY WAR LEADERS and COLONIAL LEADERS series.

Picture Credits